Teach and Learn

The First Years of Teaching

Bridget Samuel Charles

Copyright © 2024

All Rights Reserved

All rights reserved.

No part of this work may be reproduced or transmitted in any form or by any means, electronic, or mechanical, including photocopying and recording, or by any information storage or retrieval system, except as expressly permitted by the author. Request for permission can be emailed to the author at: author.bcharles@gmail.com.

Published in the United States of America
Publication Date March 2024
ISBN # 979-8-9897423-0-1

Copyright © 2024 by SamChar Publishing

Disclaimer

This book features Appendices that attempt to exemplify and explain various teaching techniques. These educational materials are protected by the Fair Use guidelines of Section 107 of the Copyright Act. All rights are reserved to the Copyright owners.

SamChar Publishing LLC

Website: samcharpublishing.com
Email: author.bcharles@gmail.com

About the Author - Bridget Samuel Charles

Bridget Samuel Charles was born on the beautiful island of Antigua in the Caribbean. She migrated to the United States, and has been an educator in New Jersey since 1990, where she taught mostly the middle grades. She has also held the position of Adjunct Professor of Humanities at a local university. Ms. Charles holds a Bachelor of Arts degree in Psychology, a Master of Arts degree in Curriculum and Instruction, and a Master of Arts degree in Educational Administration. She is married to Vaughn Charles, and currently resides in New Jersey.

Book Review

Teach and Learn - The First Year (Samuel Charles, 2024) is filled with realistic work-related examples meant to help first-year teachers, seasoned educators and school administrators become better practitioners. The author, a veteran teacher herself, encapsulates with excellent precision those enduring challenges that are most often faced by young and upcoming teachers, experienced teachers as well as school administrators. The book is filled with tested and tried as well as innovative solutions to effectively deal with students' disruptive conduct, at risk students, parents, and faculty conflicts. A well written educator's guide for elementary, middle, and high school teachers and administrators.

McChesney Emanuel, PhD
Former Principal, Former Diplomat, CEO, and Business Consultant

Table of Contents

Dedication	7
Foreword	9
Chapter 1 First Day of School - Rituals and Routines	11
Chapter 2 Getting to Know You: The First Few Weeks	17
Chapter 3 Everyone Has a Voice	23
Chapter 4 Familiarity Breeds Contempt	29
Chapter 5 Parents are Important, Too	35
Chapter 6 Tap into Colleagues	41
Chapter 7 Principals Play an Important Role	47
Chapter 8 Assessments Can Be Stressful	53
Chapter 9 Testing Is Over: Now What?	57
Chapter 10 Celebrate the Students in Several Ways	65
Chapter 11 Everybody Wins - In the Home Stretch	73
Chapter 12 It's So Hard To Say Goodbye	81
Chapter 13 You Did It! It's Time to Celebrate You	87
Afterword	93

Dedication

This book is dedicated to my mother, Elaine Gaynes Samuel, and to all the other outstanding educators who have touched my life with positivity over the years. If you are one of those teachers, you know who you are. I appreciate you deeply.

The esteemed writer, Maya Angelou, said that children do not care what you know until they know that you care. My special teachers let me know that they cared about me, and that is why they were able to draw out the best from me. They challenged me to rise even higher than I thought I could go, and for that I am thankful.

May the teachers who read this book be inspired to challenge, excite, and motivate their students to reach higher, dig deeper, and go further to achieve more than they ever dreamed of or imagined. And may they continue to stimulate their students to learn challenging new concepts with fresh enthusiasm every day.

Foreword

This book was written for teachers by a teacher. Whether you are new to the profession, or you are what is commonly referred to as a veteran, it is my hope that you will be able to glean some nuggets of valuable information from this book.

As you read, please bear in mind that the information herein is based on one person's experience in the educational system - both private and public. Yes, I have taught diverse groups of students in various settings, but there is always something new and different within this field, so my experience may not be the same as yours.

However, I bet there are some similarities to which you can relate. I hope that as you read this book, it will provide you with a reason to chuckle from time to time, and to shake your head in silent agreement. Above all else, I encourage you to carry on the brave and heroic task of educating our precious children. After all, the children are our future, aren't they?

Chapter 1

First Day of School - Rituals and Routines

The first day of school is always special. Everyone comes to school with something on their mind. Teachers are jittery because they have been in vacation mode for the past several weeks, and now they must adjust to school mode. They hope to not forget to complete any item on their mental and physical checklist of things to prepare ahead of time. Students are nervous because most of them are in a brand-new grade level with a new teacher whom some of them have not yet met or interacted with. Others have just moved into the school district from another part of the state and have no idea what to expect from this completely new school and teacher. Some new students have recently moved to this state from another state, while others have moved to the United States from another country. Some students do not even speak English!

That presents a whole new level of angst that cannot be summarily dismissed. There is a popular saying: 'He who feels it knows it'. The feelings of each of these students are real and must be considered. Does that mean that we will coddle them? Absolutely not! What it means is that educators must approach their vocation daily from the mindset that every child is an individual who presents a unique set of feelings and personality traits, much in the same way that teachers are all different, with their own individual styles and techniques for teaching.

That is why it is vitally important to be prepared for your initial year of teaching. Before the first day of school begins, it is beneficial to familiarize yourself with the culture of the students you will be teaching. Take some time to walk around the neighborhood of your prospective school. This will give you invaluable information about the demographic that you will be serving. You might even see some of your future students interacting with each other. If possible, have someone drive you around the neighborhood slowly so that you can devote your full attention to careful observation.

On the first day of school, remember that most of your students will be nervous. It is important to tread carefully, but firmly so that you set the correct tone from the beginning. The school will have its own rituals and routines, to which you will add your own as you start your day. Elementary school students are usually arranged and picked up on the playground or in the auditorium, depending on the school rules. Middle school students may be required to put away their personal effects in their lockers at the first bell and report to class by the second bell a few minutes later. Alternately, some middle schools require that students be picked up from the auditorium and escorted to their classrooms. High school students are autonomous before the start of the first period. They follow a morning routine like that of the first set of independent middle schoolers above. Having been assigned lockers, they must budget their time to include getting to their first assigned subject on time after depositing personal items in their lockers.

Whether you are teaching elementary, middle, or high school, you are the teacher and are expected to take charge of your students. Homeroom teachers in the elementary grades will have more hands-on experience with their students than teachers in the upper grades. They will not literally lay hands on the students, nor will they be in direct physical contact with them, but whereas older students are knowledgeable about school routines, elementary school students expect more step-by-step guidance from their teachers daily.

One of the first things I do on the first day of school is an icebreaker called "Getting to Know You". In this activity **(see Appendix 1)**, the children interview each other in pairs and present their peers to the rest of the class. Students ask each other a series of provided questions, the answers to which they record in preparation for presenting each other to the teacher and the class. When each child presents their partner, I record a few pertinent bits of information about each student. This helps me to quickly get into the process of getting to know my students. It also provides me with "ammunition". Why is this such a strong word? Believe it or not, the classroom can become something of a battlefield at times, and the teacher needs every advantage possible to win the war for our students' education.

There will be times when a student is not acting in accordance with what he/she expressed as his/her aspirations in life. At such times, I have a private conversation with the students and remind them of their hopes and dreams. I reiterate the specific positive things they must do to achieve their aspirations. The key word at this time is private, because it is never my intention to shame my students. It is of great importance to me that students always maintain their dignity. No matter the circumstances, the dignity of a student must be preserved intact. I use the first day of school notes throughout the school year, to affirm each child and remind them often of their stated aspirations, and how much I believe in their capability to achieve their dreams. Despite the yawning gap between aspiration and reality for many students, I believe that with a child's stated desire, the encouragement of caring adults, and good teaching skills, a student can excel beyond societal norms and/or expectations.

The Get to Know You project lasts for several hours if done in one session. This can be a bit tedious for both teachers and students. I recommend breaking it down into smaller chunks if it is a large class. I usually break the ice breaker into two parts, with the creation of rules and consequences in between. I build anticipation for each segment, so that the children look forward to hearing about their classmates and that each child is made to feel important when it is their turn to share or introduce.

On the first day of school, it is critically important to create the class rules and consequences. If truth be fully told, it is the teacher who creates these rules, but she does it with the class so craftly that the students believe they have created their own set of rules. When students take ownership of their class discipline guidelines, it is a major step in classroom management for the teacher. When needed, she can remind them how important it is to follow their self-created rules as they progress through the school year together.

One very important thing to keep in mind when formulating class rules is that they must be positive. An example of a set of class rules can be found in **Appendix 2**. Instead of "No running in the halls", that rule could be turned around to state "We always walk when moving in the halls". Instead of "No yelling out answers", the rule could be "Raise your hand and wait to be acknowledged before answering a question". Another important point to note when creating rules is that there should only be a few: no more than 4 or 5. Too many rules defeat the purpose and can overwhelm the students. The last rule should always be something like 'Obey the teacher at all times'.

I learned this success strategy from a revered and wise principal who is now deceased. His legacy lives on, as I have gleaned many nuggets of wisdom from him during my tenure at that particular school. When the final rule denotes always following the teacher's instructions, it becomes a win-win situation for the teacher. That final rule is an umbrella rule for all the other rules. Since the teacher would instruct the students to follow all the class rules, it is logical to conclude that if they break any of the other class rules, they have most definitely broken the last rule.

Along with the creation of the class rules come the consequences. As I remind my students every year, 'A rule without consequences has zero value.' It is just a group of words on paper. ' To validate a rule, one must attach a consequence for breaking the rule, and the consequence must be enforced. The consequence should reflect the seriousness of the infraction. For example, for the first violation of a rule, the consequence could be a verbal reprimand. For a repeat infraction of that rule, this could be followed by a few minutes of lunch detention. Escalating consequences could include a teacher-student conference, a call home to alert the parents of continuous breaking of school rules, a parent-teacher conference, an after-school detention, a referral to the guidance counselor, or a referral to the dean of discipline. Most students regulate their behavior after the first or second intervention technique but be prepared that there will be a very few students who will test your love of teaching by repeatedly breaking school and class rules.

It is important to establish your class rules on the first day. These should be written clearly on the board and permanently displayed in the classroom on lined chart paper or other means of display. Anyone entering your classroom must be able to see your class rules prominently displayed, and so must your students. Remember that rules are not merely written for display on a beautifully bordered poster. Rules must be followed to allow teaching and learning to occur daily, and consequences must be in place and enforced.

Once you have achieved these two goals on the first day, you have achieved a major milestone. These simple activities are the foundation upon which your school year will be built. You cannot cover all the rituals and routines on the first day; it would be overwhelming to the students and would defeat the purpose of chunking their introduction to the new class. It might even discourage some. There will be another day and another opportunity to assimilate new activities/guidelines that will be added gradually during the first week or so.

Reassure students who are overwhelmed that it takes time to become familiar with the new routines and curriculum of the class. Remind them that everyone is experiencing something new in this class. Above all else, introduce them to the saying that a journey of a thousand miles begins with the first step. Remember to stay calm and collected as you interact with your class during these first few days. Do not exhibit even a hint of nervousness, even if that is how you are feeling. Children are very perceptive, and they will discern your mood and respond in a like manner, so be firm, yet reassuring and kind. With the teacher skillfully guiding students daily, they will have no choice but to be successful as they progress confidently through the school year.

Chapter 2

Getting to Know You: The First Few Weeks

The students will become used to their new class very quickly. After the first few days, they will know exactly where to line up in the morning, how to go to the lunchroom, and how to prepare for the dismissal. This will not happen by magic. The teacher must spend time introducing and practicing each new concept to ensure mastery by the students. At first, students might feel overwhelmed. They will probably complain to their parents about all the new rules and regulations that this new teacher demands. Be prepared for that. When complaints or concerns arise from the parents during the first few days, assure them that you have everything under control and that you need them to be patient and supportive for the first few weeks. When the students see that the parents are working with the teacher and are not stressed out, they too will relax and learn the school/class rules. In all likelihood, the rules are not new. Unless this is a Pre-Kindergarten or Kindergarten classroom, students have encountered similar rules in the past, but are now flustered because they are applied in a different way in a new class and with a new teacher.

One very important routine that students must learn is how to get ready to leave the classroom. The teacher must signal that time is coming for lunch, an assembly, or dismissal. Once the signal is given, the students know it is time to pack up the learning materials and get ready. One signal used by some schools is 'STAR'. This is an acronym that helps students become quiet and attentive. When the teacher says 'STAR' **(See Appendix 3)**, students sit up straight at their desk with hands clasped, they track the speaker, and stay on task, and they respect the rules through active listening.

Now that everyone is paying attention, the teacher must take control of the attention of her students. They will be sitting attentively waiting for further instructions. Whatever routine the teacher wants to establish for the school year must be created and practiced faithfully during the first few weeks of school. At this point, the teacher can instruct her students how to proceed to get ready to leave the classroom. Whether in a row or individually, the students will leave their seats according to the teacher's instructions. A line leader is usually a good idea, and the teacher will decide how best to select one.

As they proceed out into the hallway toward their destination, there is another acronym, HALL! - which they must bear in mind **(See Appendix 4)**. Attention to this acronym enables the teacher to establish good control of her students outside of the classroom. HALL! should also be followed as students line up in the auditorium or on the playground. Students are required to walk in line with their hands at their sides, all eyes facing, lips zipped, and legs walking safely. These rules can be modified slightly for older children, but no matter their age, it is important for students to pay attention in the classroom and while walking quietly and purposefully in the hallways.

It is during these initial weeks that class leaders will emerge, and the teacher will form her first opinion of each student. This will be the time to perform diagnostic tests to establish a baseline for each student. Whatever you do as a new teacher, do not approach other teachers during the first few weeks of school asking for information about the behavior of your students in previous classes. This is a very dangerous thing to do, as it could cause you to form unfair opinions about the children in your care. It is best to interact with your students and form personal opinions and not those of others. There have been many times in my career when I have established a good reputation with a student whom other teachers had already written off as "hopeless" or "unable to learn". I have had colleagues ask me in amazement, "How did you get him to sit still long enough to write?" "Did he write that essay on his own?" "Are you a magician? He never wrote anything for me during the whole time he was with me last year. How did you do it?" I smile and reply, "I let him know that I care about him and that I have faith in him". Letting children know that you care about them builds their self-esteem. And that is the key to student success.

There are many adults today who, except for a teacher who believed in them, would not have been successful in life. Take the time to research some of the top performing business tycoons, and you will be surprised to find out that they were below par in school. Some were told that they could not learn, while others heard words like 'You'll never do well in school'. Walt Disney was told that he lacked imagination!

I advise you to make some time to get to know your students, and you will reap the benefits throughout the school year. One of my winning strategies during my years of active teaching in the classroom was to have lunch with small groups of students and get to know them on a more individual basis. I would refer to my first day-of-school peer information sheets and ask the students to elaborate on one or two of their more interesting responses. Of course, the students would also ask me questions so that they could get to know me better.

One very important area to develop during the first weeks of school is instilling in students the importance of making the best effort to do well, whether it be completing classwork and homework. However, to excel, students need adequate school supplies. There are many organizations that provide school supplies to underprivileged students at the beginning of the school year. Students can get these supplies if they qualify. However, even though some parents can afford to buy the required supplies, that is not always a priority. Some parents would much rather buy expensive designer shoes than daily school supplies. It would be a good idea for you to have extra notebooks, pens, and pencils in the classroom for your students who lack these supplies. Office supply stores have back-to-school sales just before the start of school, with deep discounts for teachers. I would suggest stocking up on staples. Yes, you will have to buy several required items out of your own pocket, but that is the price we pay as teachers to facilitate daily learning.

In previous years, I have provided students with food, notebooks, pencils, pens, crayons, markers, gym uniforms, regular school uniforms, sweaters, winter coats, and even dress clothing for special performances. It is simply what we do as teachers. We are surrogate parents. I learned this from a previous principal who taught that we are *in loco parentis*, which means that we take the place of their parents when our students are in our care. We are called to nurture them and provide a positive, stimulating, and inviting learning environment. Who can learn on an empty stomach or when shivering from the cold? We must empathize with our students. And that is why, when they need us for whatever valid reason, we rise to the occasion. Teaching is our superpower.

Bridget Samuel Charles

Chapter 3

Everyone Has a Voice

Yes, everyone has a voice that must be heard. As an educator, you must realize that people are different in various ways, but one thing we all have in common is our voice. Some people use theirs loudly and try to drown out what others have to say, while others timidly cower in the corner, hoping that no one notices them. You find these people in many groups, especially at school. In a typical group of students, there will be the self-proclaimed "overachiever" who will loudly brag about their accomplishments. You will most likely find hard working students who do not need to blow their own horn, and you can be certain that in a group there will be at least one student who lacks the courage or self-confidence to speak up and state their opinion on any given subject.

Too often, these students are overlooked by teachers, and, through the ripple effect, they get lost in the shuffle and consequently, the entire class suffers. Why do I say the ripple effect? Well, due to the exclusion of some students with low self-esteem, the class will not achieve the excellent grades they could have achieved with better teacher facilitation. Too often, bossy students create an environment within both the whole group and during small group instruction that does not invite everyone to share. They are allowed to establish an unwritten rule that their opinion is the only one that counts. If someone who is not as articulate as they try to voice an opinion, they shoot it down. If someone is tentative in their speech because their ideas do not flow as easily or as quickly as it does for the overachiever, they are greeted with smirks and other forms of silent, and sometimes overt, derision. These students soon learn that their opinions do not matter, and so they stop sharing in class. Because they are unable to exchange ideas in the group, some children shut down and block out the current concept, irrespective of its importance. When it comes to the comprehension assessment of the students, the class average scores are lower than they should or could be. Sometimes the teacher becomes frustrated with the test results, but if she/he were to do some active research regarding what is happening in the classroom, she/he would realize that the ripple effect prevents maximum class achievement. There is an acronym, TEAM, which means Together Everyone Achieves More. When everyone's voice is not heard in groupwork, a critical piece of the education fabric is lost. That is why it is so important for the teacher to observe her students, to listen attentively, and to conduct one-on-one interviews from time to time. As she monitors the class during whole-group and small-group instruction, she should be on guard to ensure that everyone's voice is heard.

Take, for example, Malcolm, who was a seventh-grade special education student whom I met when I was hired as a seventh-grade teacher a couple of months before the end of the school year. Malcolm had been told over the years that he was not smart enough and that his voice did not matter. He was not told this in so many words, but the attitude of his teachers throughout the years and the treatment by other students told him in no uncertain terms that his voice did not matter, that he could not read well and that he certainly could not write good stories. When I first met Malcolm, it broke my heart to realize what had happened to him over the years. He was broken. You could see the resignation on his face acknowledging the fact that he had nothing to contribute to the class. He was silent during discussions and never raised his hand to volunteer an answer to any question.

Yes, Malcolm was a special education student, but that did not mean that he could not learn. The previous teachers needed to make accommodations in the way they delivered the curriculum to Malcolm, but he could learn. And, in truth, after interacting with Malcolm, I acknowledged that he may never become an A student, but he could improve from his current situation, which was not his best effort. Malcolm had shifted his learning motor into low gear, but with greater self-confidence and determination, he could be encouraged to optimize his potential and might even achieve passing grades. However, he had to see the value in making the effort to succeed in that class.

Suffice it to say that I adjusted my teaching style to accommodate Malcolm. I gave him extra time, encouraged him to always speak out and praised him for his efforts whenever he did. By the end of the semester, which was also the end of the school year, Malcolm was writing regularly in English Language Arts class and was confidently volunteering to share his ideas, though speaking hesitantly at times. His writing, though below the average for the class, was much more than he had ever done before. Malcolm was not at the proficiency level yet, but he had made considerable progress and was well on his way.

The next year I stayed with that class, so I was their 8th grade homeroom teacher. I continued to teach English Language Arts, and I am very proud to say that Malcolm was able to graduate with his class at the end of that year. He needed a considerable amount of one-on-one attention, but I worked closely with his Special Education Inclusion teacher, and he put forth the extra effort for which we both knew he had the potential. Malcolm has gone on to be a self-employed mechanic after attending and graduating from a vocational high school and a training institute geared to his interest. Saying I am proud of him and his achievements is an understatement.

Too often teachers allow bright students to subtly bully others, like Malcolm, into submission to the dominant student's will. During whole group and small group instruction, a teacher must be vigilant. Watch and listen as the students interact with each other. Do not allow students to put each other down. A teacher must sit in small groups and monitor what is happening so that any problems can be nipped in the bud. Everyone deserves to learn in an inviting and supportive environment **(See Appendix 7)**. Group work is shared work, and everyone's voice must be heard before a group decision is made. School is not just for some students; it is for all, and teachers must nurture every student. As human beings, we instinctively gravitate to bright and articulate students, but as educators, we must take the time to also work with less confident people who hesitate to share ideas because they lack self-esteem. They are afraid that they will be laughed at and/or humiliated if they give the wrong answer.

Another time when a teacher must work intentionally to ensure that everyone's voice is heard is during whole group instruction. Whether reviewing a concept or checking for comprehension of new information, a teacher should not allow one or a few students to dominate the class. Yes, that bright student knows the answers to all the questions, but they must be made to listen to the opinions of others. In many cases, it is not just a right or wrong answer to the question. No matter the subject area, open-ended questions require a justification for the answer. If only a few students are allowed to answer, that negates the idea of hearing every student's voice. No, not every student will be able to answer every question out loud due to time constraints, but we can get feedback from everyone using a variety of strategies.

Within the entire group, students can be asked to respond using techniques such as Think-Pair-Share, The Idea Wave, **(See Appendix 5 and 6)** or by using popsicle sticks and randomly pulling students' names. Everyone may not feel comfortable sharing in the whole group at first but given the time and encouragement of the teacher and peers, students' confidence will increase. Some of the shyest students will become the boldest and most outspoken. This will ultimately be reflected in improved overall scores. However, it all starts with the teacher, the instructional leader in the classroom, setting the tone, and establishing the protocol for discussions. Once this is in place, all stakeholders will understand and appreciate the unwritten rule that everyone's voice must be heard, and everyone must be respected.

A word of advice when praising students: do it in a concrete way. Praise their action, and do not constantly use a general praise phrase such as, "Good Job!", "Nice Work!", or "Great!". Let the child know exactly what he/she did correctly. You could say something like, "I admire how John corrected himself when he answered that question. It shows me that he is thinking about his answer. Good reasoning skills, John." You may also say something like, "What a great suggestion, Mia. That's another way of looking at it." A teacher could also say, "The Obama Group is doing a good job discussing the question before deciding on a group answer," or "Briana provided text support for her answer. Way to go, Briana!" When students know exactly what they are being praised for, they will be encouraged to participate more in class activities.

Chapter 4

Familiarity Breeds Contempt

Don't Mistake My Kindness for Weakness!

One very grave mistake that some new teachers make is to become too familiar with their students. They rationalize this familiarity by thinking they want their students to like them. Huge mistake! You don't want your students to merely like you; you want them to also respect you. If you aim for respect, it will come through. Your students will also like you, and they will adhere to the parameters you have set. Children will go as far as you allow them. The saying 'Fences make good neighbors' also applies to education.

Teachers should be friendly to their students, but they should understand that they are not students' friends. This is an area that causes many new teachers to lose control, respect, and obedience from their students. Classroom management is the axis upon which everything else in the classroom rests and around which they rotate. Setting boundaries early in the school year will benefit both the teacher and students and can very well determine the teacher's success or failure for that school year.

This chapter is titled "Familiarity Breeds Contempt" and it could not be truer if I invented the saying myself. When a teacher allows her students to become too familiar, it becomes detrimental in more ways than one. Students will physically invade the teacher's private space and will not necessarily obey instructions they consider unimportant. Examples of this would be students leaving the lunch line to walk over and run their fingers through the teacher's long hair, or they might stroke the teacher's arm while waiting to be seated in the auditorium for a special performance. One might argue that it does not hurt anyone if the children touch the teacher, but it is simply not the right thing to do, especially in these times of physical and sexual abuse allegations and the need for safe sanctuaries.

I worked with a male teacher once who was accused of sexually abusing a female student. He denied the charges vehemently, but his reputation had become so tarnished by the mere allegation of abuse, and the whispers of everyone who knew about the situation that he was traumatized. He tried to take his own life and, according to the rumor mill at the time, he had to be put into a mental institution. That man, who was an exemplary teacher before the incident, has lost his teaching license and will never be a teacher again.

Who was telling the truth? The student alleged that the teacher would bring her to the classroom during lunch for additional lessons. They would be in the classroom alone with the door closed, and he would use that opportunity to accost her sexually. Only those two individuals know for sure what happened in the classroom during those sessions. He maintained his innocence, stating that he was kindhearted in offering her extra help with her lessons, because she was failing. The student maintained that he sexually abused her. While some folks condemn the teacher, others believe that the student took advantage of his kindness to cover up her academic failure. All of that could have been avoided if the teacher had brought two or three other students, and above all else, if he had let the classroom door remain open during their lunchtime tutoring sessions.

Teachers should keep physical contact with students to a minimum. There may be a time when a student is out of school for an extended period for whatever reason, and when they return, they are so overcome with emotion that they run towards and hug their teacher. A brief hug in a situation like that may be tolerated, and might even be warranted, but hugs should not be initiated by the teacher.

Children, especially the younger ones, are very impressionable, and do not always know when and where to draw the line about displays of affection. My mother used to always say, "When you give a child an inch, they will try to take a mile." Again, we must establish boundaries that shall never be crossed. Yes, we love our students in a platonic way, but as educators, we are about the business of teaching and learning, and that must be the focus at school. We cannot afford to even give the impression of impropriety in our daily interactions with our students. Some parents are very litigious, and are constantly on the lookout for reasons to sue teachers.

Our yes must be yes, and our no must be no. Is there any wiggle room? Of course, but first you have to establish your reputation as a fair, caring, yet firm educator. When I was a new teacher, I had a reputation for being kind and nice, so one student decided to take advantage of me. What he did not know was that I was also known for being firm. This first-grade boy, whom I will call John, was known as a runner, but being new to the school, I did not know that. John did not realize that my no meant no. The class was having recess on the playground, and soon it was time to go back inside. John decided that he wanted to go home. He said he was tired of being at school. I gently told him: "No, John. It is time to go back inside. You will go home later." I spoke reassuringly to him. I think John heard me, because he nodded as he looked at me. He stood there silently on the line until I turned and gave the signal to the line leader to start walking inside. As soon as my back was turned, John ran away. The class erupted into screams to get my attention as he ran out of the playground perimeter, and headed toward the street. I sized up the situation quickly, and ran after John. It took a little while, but I caught up with him, my heart beating wildly.

John was not about to stop on his own, so I had to grab him. First, I grabbed his arm, but he quickly whisked it away. I was terrified that he would run headlong into traffic and be hurt or even killed. After several unsuccessful attempts, I grabbed John's sweater and uniform shirt collar, and was able to stop him in a flash of time from going into the path of a speeding car on the busy street. Unfortunately, when I grabbed John, my fingernails scratched his neck. After returning to the classroom, I alerted the principal to what had happened outside, and completed the necessary incident report to document John's escapade.

Later that day, while working in the After School program, John's grandmother came to the school screaming about child abuse, stating that John had several marks on his body to prove that I had abused him. After calmly explaining the situation to John's grandmother, she understood what had happened and started berating her grandson for his unruly behavior. Thanks to the eyewitness accounts of my other students and fellow teachers who were on the playground at the time, I was exonerated. But what if I didn't have witnesses? That is why it is extremely important to be businesslike and firm with your students and to love and care about them dearly, but from a distance.

Some children mistake your kindness for weakness, and some others become confused when recalling classroom incidents. I had to rely on my reputation and witnesses to get me out of a sticky situation when I had a mentally challenged boy named Aaron in my fifth-grade class. Aaron alleged that I had beat him up because he gave the wrong answer to a question. I was in complete shock when I heard this allegation against me. Thankfully, the other students were able to verify what had happened on the day in question. It turns out that Aaron was embarrassed because he had given an answer that was totally unrelated to the question and the class laughed at him. I admonished the students right away and sternly forbade them from making fun of him. Somehow, Aaron internalized that incident to mean that I was the bad guy, and he formulated a complete scenario of physical abuse.

That day, he went home and told his version of the story to his father, who came to school the next day and complained. Fortunately, I was able to explain the situation to Aaron's father, who quickly realized that his son had made up the whole story. I put that matter to rest and cleared my name. I don't hold any grudge against Aaron. I wish him all the best and hope that he has since received the help he needed to distinguish between fantasy and reality. Once again, I documented the incident, thus creating a paper trail to protect my reputation. I think about that bizarre allegation occasionally.

Again, it is very important to have witnesses when interacting with a child one-on-one. A teacher should never ever be alone in a room with a single child. Even if a child is mandated to report to you in the classroom for whatever reason, make sure there are two others present, in case you need witnesses. No teacher should be punished for being kind; they must keep in mind that familiarity breeds contempt and be proactive. Too often, it is one person's word against another, which causes problems, sometimes resulting in suspension of a teacher or even termination. To avoid this, teachers must put into practice the saying "Be as wise as a serpent, but as harmless as a dove".

Chapter 5

Parents are Important, Too

As you work your way through the school year, you will quickly realize the importance of parents in the education of our students. After all, they are the children's first teachers, so they know them very well, and will have valuable tips to share with teachers. Parents can be a great benefit to teachers, and teachers must be clever enough to understand how to use them as partners in education.

I would advise you to get to know the parents of your students as quickly as possible. They will be an asset to you. You cannot do the job of educating your students by yourself. You need others, including parents, to be a very important part of the world of education. It is vital to cultivate good relationships with your students' parents. Of course, you must be always professional, but you must let the parents know how much you care for their children. From the Open House at the beginning of the school year, to parent-teacher conferences, from the school concerts and field trips to the end-of-year/graduation events, parents should be involved and must be made to understand that their role is important.

Most first meetings between the homeroom teacher and the parents occur either on the first day of school or at the Open House, sometimes referred to as Back-to-School Night, a week or two into the school year. It is important for the teacher to make a good impression on the parents. It is even more important for the teacher and parents to foster a good working relationship. I would not advise pretending to be someone you are not when you meet your students' parents. Simply be yourself and keep the meeting friendly, yet businesslike. Parents detest pretension and appreciate authenticity, so be your authentic self; again, do not pretend to be more experienced or qualified than you are.

At the Open House, I usually address parents as a group before meeting with the parents of individual students, and I encourage them to sit in their child's seat during the meeting. I highly recommend using Power Point or other digital presentations. Introduce yourself and state your expectations for the year. Every parent will not attend the Open House, and some will arrive late to the meeting for various reasons, including having multiple children in the school. Be patient and be prepared to repeat some information as needed. Have copies of an introductory/welcome letter from the teacher and the required supply list, as well as the class rules and consequences, ready in the parent packet that will have been prepared ahead of time. A private letter from the child to his/her parents is always a welcome addition to the Open House packet. I also encourage teachers to inform parents about the rewards systems in place in the classroom.

Once your entire group presentation is completed and you have answered parents' questions and addressed their concerns, invite parents to browse through the classroom and review their child's work, which should be available in their desk and/or on a bulletin board. Keep in mind that the Open House is not a parent-teacher conference, but if there are any pressing concerns from parents, you should address them. Additionally, you can use this opportunity to speak with any parent whose child's behavior is of concern. Be as discreet as possible. Do not discuss a child within the hearing of other parents.

Remember, as you are interacting with the parents, they are sizing you up and forming their own opinion of you. You will soon learn which parents will be the best field trip chaperones, which are supportive and which parents are critical and unhelpful. Bear in mind that first impressions are not always correct, so be prepared to get to know your parents better before forming concrete opinions. Meanwhile, greet everyone with a positive attitude and regard all of them as allies.

One of the most important times you will interact with parents will be during parent-teacher conferences. Formal conferences occur multiple times throughout the school year, but you can have a conference with a parent whenever the need arises. To prepare for the conference, I created a **Parent-Teacher Conference Log.** I complete a log for each child ahead of time to utilize the precious 15-minute conference time expeditiously **(See Appendix 8)**. On this form, students are evaluated in two categories: social and academic, and in each category, I discuss their strengths and challenges. There is always space left on the form for comments from the parents. At the end of the conference, both the parent and the teacher sign and date the form to verify the contents of the conference log, and the parent receives a copy. Conducting your conference in in this way not only saves time, but it shows great respect to parents, as you offer them the opportunity to make comments.

Over the years, I have heard many parents exclaim in surprise and admiration about the use of my conference log.

They are especially happy to be able to retain a copy for their records. The conference log performs four important functions:

1. It enables a teacher to establish and maintain good written communication with the parents of their students.
2. It enables teachers to document any behavior concerns and to praise students' performance.
3. Provides parents with written documentation of their child's progress in school in an easy-to-read format.
4. It affords parents the opportunity to give a written response to the teacher's comments during that meeting.

The conference log has been one of the most valuable documents in my possession as an educator. That is why I have shared it countless times with my colleagues and other educators and why I am sharing it with you now.

School concerts and field trips are other events that require working closely with parents. I have benefited over the years from cultivating good working relationships with parents who could be relied on to help with the rehearsals and wardrobe for concerts, or to accompany the class on field trips. Most school event destinations require a specific ratio of adult chaperones to children, and teachers are sometimes left floundering at the last minute to meet the requirements. When you have reliable parents, that is one headache that that you can avoid.

I have been very fortunate to have had excellent parents each year in the areas of cooperation and willingness to volunteer. In retrospect, I think they were average parents at first, but became excellent after they got to know me and realized that I had their children's best interests at heart. Parents, like children, don't care about what you know, or how many degrees you possess, until you show them that you care about their children. Once you have done that, it is my experience that those parents will do anything to make your teaching experience smoother and more enjoyable. You can ask for favors from them, even make requests without prior notice, and they will be happy to oblige.

As teachers, we must choose daily between being kind or mean-spirited. It should not be a difficult decision. We must choose to be kind. Parents are people too, and as such they must be respected and appreciated. It does not take much from us to let the parents know how much we appreciate them. Above all else, showing appreciation to parents creates good will, which will trickle down to our relationships with the students. When a child realizes that his/her mother or father is working closely with the teacher as a partner in his/her education, he/she will be even further motivated to learn. When a child sees respect as the common factor between his/her parents and teacher, he/she will also be respectful. The opposite is also true: When a child realizes that his parents do not respect his teacher, or his teacher speaks disrespectfully about his parents, he is less likely to cooperate in the learning environment. Choosing to be kind every day has many benefits, including improved relationships, and that is why it is vitally important to regard parents as important partners in education.

Teachers, we have a huge job to do. It may be daunting at times, but it is doable, and it can be enjoyable as well. When we teach, we must also be willing to learn from our students, from our colleagues, from our administrators, and yes, even from the parents of our students. Teaching is a unique and honorable profession that enables us to change lives for better or worse. It is the only profession that affects all other professions in the world. We must choose what we say and do wisely, and be intentional about how we interact with others, because when we teach, we touch lives and affect the future forever.

Chapter 6

Tap into Colleagues

I cannot say it loudly enough or often enough how important it is to have a good working relationship with colleagues. There is a saying that no man is an island. Human beings are social creatures, and as such, we rely on each other for success. No one succeeds by herself or fails by herself. When we get the full realization of that concept, we will be well on our way to lifelong success.

Teachers are a unique set of individuals. In general, we think of each other by last name. Although I am a female, many people associate me with the name Charles. Educators can spend their entire career working with other teachers and never call them by their first name. This does not mean that they are less close to their coworkers than in any other profession. However, since we must call each other Mr. so and so or Ms. so and so in front of the children, we just maintain that protocol throughout. I have been addressed as "Charles" many times by colleagues, not "Ms. Charles" or "Bridget", and I don't take offense. There is no disrespect intended, and no disrespect is taken. That is just the way we are as teachers.

Novice teachers are strongly advised to show respect for older, more experienced teachers. They are the ones who will mentor you, give you sound advice, and intervene to defend you, whether from parents or other educators, when necessary. Veteran teachers are usually willing to model teaching strategies for novice teachers, and will share bulletin board ideas and classroom management skills when needed. They will share with you the benefits of having a growth mindset, as opposed to a fixed mindset. Experienced teachers might even share information regarding the importance of pacing your lessons correctly for the seamless delivery of the curriculum. They will remind you that effective pacing helps a teacher hold the students' attention, and affords a balance in instruction so that students will be at optimal learning. You can learn a lot of practical information from veteran teachers, so my advice is to befriend them, be coachable, and above all else, be respectful to them. There is a saying that you will catch more flies with honey than with vinegar, and that is true. Studies show that people are more productive in a positive environment.

Of course, you will not gravitate toward everyone in the same way, and every veteran teacher is not warm and friendly. You cannot be responsible for anyone else, but you must be responsible for yourself. Despite how your colleague appears at the first meeting, continue to be respectful and kind. You may have heard of "killing them with kindness". In other words, as you continue to be kind, you will overcome even the toughest barriers. You may never become close friends with many of your co-workers, but they will respect you for your kindness and your generous spirit. And kindness will be the portal through which favors will come.

One of your colleagues may have previously been the homeroom teacher of a class in your current grade level, or they may have taught some of your current students the previous year. That teacher can help or hinder you. However, you should not ask colleagues to tell you about their experiences with the individual students before meeting the students, because it is of optimum importance that you form your own opinions. However, fellow teachers can provide invaluable information on how to effectively deliver the curriculum. Veteran teachers can tell you what strategies worked and what didn't, and how they implemented the winning techniques.

When I started working in what is called the "inner city" in the public school system, I was outside my league in no uncertain terms. I could not relate to many of the children, having never lived in the inner city, having only taught previously in the Catholic School system in the USA, and having been born and raised in another country. However, I was coachable; I was willing to learn from veteran teachers. I was fine for the first couple of years or so. At the end of the second year, I patted myself on the back and enjoyed my summer vacation. I prepared for the upcoming new school year, blissfully unaware that I was about to be tested.

That year, I faced a major challenge that proved the importance of tapping into colleagues. One of my students, Donald, performed at the higher end of my class academically. I could usually rely on him to raise his hand to ask and answer questions and to volunteer answers and opinions to open-ended questions. He was consistently reliable in whole group and small group settings and was regarded by his classmates as a leader. I was pleased with Donald's performance until one day when it seemed as if someone had flipped a switch that controlled him.

Donald was a different student at school that day. He was withdrawn and brooding and appeared depressed and angry as he sat with his head face down at his desk. Whenever I tried to involve him in the lesson, he would utter kurt and sometimes monosyllabic responses. I was puzzled and concerned, but I did not want to embarrass him in front of everyone. It is my personal policy to always ensure the dignity of my students, so I asked Donald to step outside the classroom door for a private one-on-one conference, while the other students wrote the answer to an open question.

When I asked him what was wrong today, he barked at me that he was fine, all the while with an angry expression on his face. Once I realized that he would not provide any more information, we rejoined the class. I racked my brains unsuccessfully to come up with the reasons for Donald's bizarre behavior. That night I called his home, and Donald's mother assured me that he was fine. There was not much else I could do.

The next day in class, it was as if the switch had been turned back on. Donald was himself once again. He participated in class, and was pleasant to his classmates and me. I did not question that. I was happy to have my best-performing student back.

This behavior occurred a few more times over the next few months, and I was at my wits' end to find out the root cause of Donald's problem. One day, I spoke to the "gym" teacher as I picked up my students from the gymnasium after Physical Education class. I reckoned that he was male and had more experience teaching Donald than I. As soon as I mentioned the problem of Donald appearing to be Dr. Jekyll and Mr. Hyde, the teacher told me exactly what was happening to cause this bizarre behavior. Apparently, Donald was experiencing severe problems at home with his parents, to the point that the Division of Youth and Family Services (DYFS) had just become involved. His unusual behavior on certain days mirrored the days when he was abused at home.

Armed with this new knowledge, I was able to tailor my instruction to be more understanding of Donald on days when he was unresponsive and withdrawn. He was able to remain with the class until the end of the school year, but thanks to the information from a veteran colleague, I understood what was happening to my student at home and was able to make modifications to our learning environment. Donald was eventually taken out of the home of his parents and placed with his maternal grandmother for his own safety and overall well-being.

The story of Donald is only one of several in which more experienced veteran teachers have helped me over the years. If I were not coachable, they would be less willing to help. My mother was also a highly respected educator, and one of the things she taught me was that we should always give respect where and when it is due. Novice teachers must respect those who are more experienced. They have "been there and done that" as the saying goes, and they can help you through difficult situations if you are willing to learn from them. Many veterans are ready and willing to help, but the novice must have the right attitude and be receptive to critique and advice. We all work for the good of our students, so everyone should be willing to unite and help each other. Remember that there is no I in TEAM.

When a new, inexperienced teacher is hired in a public school district, they are usually assigned a mentor, a veteran teacher who will help guide them during their first year at that school. I would advise you to take full advantage of this opportunity to learn from someone who is more experienced overall and who is familiar with your current school. This teacher will pay periodic visits to your classroom sometimes just to pop in and say hi, and sometimes to observe and critique your teaching. The key word here is critique. Their purpose is not to tear you down. Instead, they will help you become the master teacher you were designed to be. Respect your mentor. Take notes as they advise you. You will be surprised at the strong friendship that can develop from this random assignment to each other.

Just as someone mentors you when you are inexperienced, you in turn should mentor new teachers as you gain expertise in your teaching craft. Your mentees will thank you, and will pass on whatever knowledge you impart to them when they eventually become veterans. I stay in touch with my mentor and mentees as much as possible, and it is a great feeling to be part of the fabric of the United States educational system. When colleagues work together, they establish strong relationships, and students benefit. And that is what education is all about.

Chapter 7

Principals Play an Important Role

One of the most important relationships you will foster throughout your career is the one with your current principal. As with any other career, there are mediocre, good, and great principals. There are even a few principals who are inept - not good at doing their job. Let us be realistic. Some principals are the product of nepotism, and being incompetent in that position, the students ultimately suffer. However, for the purpose of this book, we will focus on positivity: on good and great principals who take their responsibilities seriously and guide their staff daily to greatness.

A good principal is a role model. He/She will nurture you in such a way that you are encouraged to return to school the next day "bright-eyed and bushy-tailed". In essence, the principal is your biggest cheerleader. As the instructional leader in the school, it is their job to set the tone for the learning environment. A good principal will help you to be proficient, but a great principal raises the bar and not only encourages you, but empowers you to excel and become highly proficient.

Children are not the only ones who need encouragement every day. Adults need it as well. A principal's words to a novice teacher can be like a cup of cool water to a parched throat on a hot summer day. I am not referring to hollow words spoken by a principal to flatter a teacher, while not supporting them in any tangible way. Instead, the great principal is intentional about his/her word choice in giving praise and is not prone to flattery. He/She ensures that teachers have access to necessary resources and puts measures in place to ensure that those resources are utilized expeditiously. The great principal has an open-door policy, thereby assuring new teachers that they are not alone; that help is easily accessible, and that the teacher's efforts are appreciated.

It is of paramount importance for teachers to always remember that the principal-teacher relationship is just that. It is a professional relationship that should not be tainted by close personal friendship, at least not while working under the supervision of that principal. A teacher must learn to compartmentalize his/her life to a certain extent, and to interact with colleagues and supervisors appropriately. That is an important key to successful working relationships. A principal cannot and must not be primarily your friend. He/She is there to do the job of promoting learning in the school, first and foremost. Any distraction from that will result in sub-par student achievements. If we are all on the same page, we will realize that the students' best interests must take precedence over personal feelings and relationships.

Teachers can tap into their principal as they continue to grow in pedagogy and daily experience with students. A good principal genuinely wants to know how the teacher's year is going, and what he/she can do to facilitate the faculty member's experience. Be friendly to the principal but know where to draw the line. Once you have established that line of cordiality, great ideas can be exchanged, and your year will be off to a great start.

What you should not do is complain to the principal for every minor problem. The principal is not there to solve all your problems. You, as the instructional leader in your own classroom, must find solutions to minor problems. There is a saying, "See three, before me." This can apply to how you approach your visits to the principal's office. Consult other faculty members before bombarding the principal with your problems. Talk to a mentor, a grade-level lead teacher, or another trusted colleague before presenting your problem to the principal. Principals appreciate teachers who are proactive, and who are willing to brainstorm a problem before assailing the principal for solutions.

You will garner more respect from a principal if you present yourself as someone who is level-headed and rational, rather than a person who depends on others to solve classroom management issues. A principal appreciates a faculty member who not only presents a problem, when necessary, but also suggests one or two ways to solve it. If you keep your interactions with the principal respectful and friendly, you will gain favor and will be assured of having an ally when any major problems arise. You are in charge of the impression you make on the principal, so make a good one.

One very important point to remember is that the principal or vice principal who does your formal and informal observations and evaluations is not there to "get you". That individual is a professional who is committed to helping you be the best teacher you can possibly be. Do not take their suggestions for improvement personally. Remember, when you change the way you look at something, the thing you are looking at changes. Instead of thinking that your supervisor does not like you, think instead that they are challenging you to grow and develop even more in your field. They are helping you to be a better teacher.

I have had good and bad experiences with principles over the years, but the good experiences far outweigh the bad. I have had several principals who were devastated when it was time for me to move on to another position at another school, and that caused me a great deal of angst. On the one hand, I was happy to have meant so much to my principal, but on the other hand, I knew it was time to move onward and upward to forge new and exciting experiences for myself. I have had only one principal in my entire career, who made my decision to leave that school easy and worry-free.

Again, I reiterate that all principals are not the same. However, recognizing him/her as the school's instructional leader, it is important that you, the novice teacher, show her/him the respect due to the person in that position. Despite my unsavory experience with one principal, I maintained my cheerful demeanor and never lacked deference in my dealings with that person. There is a saying that when someone offends you, especially wrongfully, you should "kill them with kindness". When you do that, they will have no recourse but to be respectful and fair to you when you show them nothing but respect.

On at least three occasions, and by three different principals, I have been selected to receive prestigious awards. This would not have happened if I had had a bad attitude. Yes, my work speaks for itself, but I have seen outstanding teachers be overlooked because of their confrontational attitude toward the principal. It is not worth it to put in the hard work of managing your class and empowering your students to achieve high scores on standardized tests if you are in a constant fight with your supervisors, especially the principal. This causes stress for the teacher, which can be internalized into high blood pressure or some other serious disease that can be detrimental to you on many levels.

Stress at work can be averted by self-care. Take time to do self-care in one form or another, so that you can put your best foot forward. Self-care includes eating well, exercising, and getting enough rest at night. Getting massages periodically would also be a good idea. When you take the time to care for yourself, you will be less stressed out and will be able to establish and maintain good relationships with others, including your students and their parents, and colleagues. Being calm, pleasant, and levelheaded is particularly crucial when interacting with the principal.

When educators practice self-care, it creates a win-win situation. Learning to love yourself is the foundation for caring for others. When traveling on an airplane, the flight attendants usually instruct adult passengers who are traveling with a child to put on their oxygen mask first in case of an emergency, and then put on the mask of the child. Why? Because you will be of no help to that child if you run out of oxygen and pass out before you put on your own mask. Similarly, a teacher has to take the time to care for him/herself as she/he cultivates positive relationships with students, parents, colleagues, and the principal.

To sum it all up, the principal, the educational leader of the school, is someone who can help you hone your skills and achieve success, or who can hinder your professional growth. It is in your best interest to get along well with him/her in such a way that he/she will go to bat for you. There will be some point in your career when things may not be going your way, and you need someone in your corner. Having developed a great relationship with your principal, he/she will be your biggest cheerleader and will help you avert possible disaster.

Chapter 8

Assessments Can Be Stressful

Teachers are told not to teach to the standardized state tests, but if schools are judged by the test results, then teachers must always keep the formal tests in mind. As you go through the year delivering the curriculum, you will have many experiences, some of which will be delightful and uplifting, and some will be downright heartbreaking and depressing. For example, when you see a child showing noticeable progress in a specific area where she or he had been struggling, it brings great joy to your heart. On the other hand, when you have been working tirelessly with a child every day, have reached out to their parents to let them know that their child is failing, and you have created a peer study buddy to help the child learn additional strategies, it can be easy to feel like a failure. You may even have given that child individual tutoring, but all to no avail. The child still maintained failing or barely passing grades, despite all the accommodations and help placed before him or her.

Don't be discouraged. As heartbreaking as it is to acknowledge, you cannot reach everyone. What you can do is your best. Once you know you have put forth your best efforts, there is nothing further you can do. However, one thing you should never do is give up on a child. Sometimes a child who has not responded to the first ninety-nine attempts of presenting a concept will surprise everyone and react positively on the hundredth try. Every child is important and is worth your relentless efforts to educate them, so stay positive and keep trying.

After the spring break there is usually a period of frantic schoolwide preparation for standardized testing. This can take many forms. At one school, the principal became very involved in test preparation activities. Since each child's formal assessment grade is reflected on the school, it behooves the educators to ensure that their students perform well. This does not include direct communication with the child in the examination room. All the preparation must take place beforehand. Once the testing day arrives, the child either knows how to answer the test questions or they do not, but they must do it on their own.

Before the testing, the teachers or examiners and their assistants, Proctors, will be trained according to the rules of the state. Members of staff will be instructed regarding the testing process. They will be given all the information necessary to administer the test successfully. Once the testing starts and examples have been provided of what is expected in that section of the test, the child is on his own to calculate the correct answers or to write the essay or narrative account using the strategies that have been covered in class previously. A teacher cannot by any gesture communicate to students whether the answer is correct or incorrect. That would be tantamount to cheating, and the teacher's job would be in jeopardy.

Standardized testing should not be taken lightly. It establishes the level by which schools are judged, and as a representative of the school and state, the teacher's behavior in the testing room must reflect professionalism. There is no need for the teacher to become excessively stressed out during the testing process. There will be some level of stress, but if you follow the protocol laid out during training by the Chief Testing Administrator in your school building, all will be well. Of course, exigent circumstances can occur. That is why there are additional administrators and additional proctors constantly monitoring the hallways in some districts. They are there to provide assistance if any unusual or unexpected incidents occur. Tap into them if needed.

As a test examiner, the teacher must be the consummate professional, even more so than in the classroom every day. There can be no eye contact with the students during the actual test, no hand, or head signals, and no verbal instructions regarding the information on the students' answer sheets. The teacher will be required to give specific instructions to the students as they get ready to start the test. The entire script will be provided in the Examiner's Manual. Once the teacher has done the practice items with the students, has given the directions and stated the length of time allowed for the test, he/she will officially announce the start of the test and document same on the board, or with a digital countdown visible to everyone. The teacher is required to walk around the room to monitor the students during the entire test. He/she will also update the time remaining for the test every ten minutes.

When a child has made a selection on the answer sheet, whether it is correct or not, a teacher cannot intervene and certainly must not indicate to the student whether the chosen answer is correct. If the child is well prepared, it will be reflected in their grade, but if, for whatever reason, that child does not implement the required strategies to answer the questions correctly, his/her score will be low. At the risk of being repetitive, it is imperative that the teacher allows the students to work independently and not attempt to influence them in any way.

Recall the importance of self-care as you go through this week and keep that in mind. Make an extra effort to pamper yourself more than usual. Make sure to get enough rest at night and during the actual test. Take bathroom breaks when needed. Above all else, relax during the test and follow the guidelines provided by the school district. Take good care of yourself. Be professional. Do not provide even the slightest loophole that could cause you to be accused of impropriety. There should never be the appearance of improper behavior as you administer the test.

Be extra vigilant from the time you pick up the testing materials in the morning until you return them to the testing office every day immediately after testing. Keep a level head and follow the instructions as outlined by your supervisors. During testing, your students will notice the silent cues you emit through your body language. Model professionalism and confidence to your students. Show them a pleasant demeanor, even when you feel stressed out. Show them positive energy and integrity as you interact with them within the confines of the testing protocol. Your students will be a reflection of you and will automatically mirror your positive attitude. With you as their role model, they will try their best, and whatever the test results may be, for that week all will be well.

Chapter 9

Testing Is Over: Now What?

Testing is over and life goes on. Administrators expect to continue the education process with teaching and learning taking place, but your students will become antsy. As they sense that they are getting closer to the end of the school year than to the beginning, their restlessness intensifies. Once you have passed the halfway mark around the middle of February, there will be some challenges to come, and this becomes more evident after the spring break.

Think of the school year as a mountain. In early September, everyone comes to school bright-eyed and bushy-tailed, ready to take on the challenge of the upcoming school year. In this analogy, you are starting to climb the mountain. Between the months of September and January, you are continuously ascending, striving to reach the mountain peak. By early to mid-February, you reach the summit and can look back and get a glimpse of the distance that you have come so far, but you are aware that the journey is not over.

Testing week usually occurs at some point during the last weeks of March and the early weeks of April, depending on the parameters set forth by the State of New Jersey or by whatever state where the students reside. At this juncture, there is a common belief among some students that because the hard work of climbing or test preparation is over, they can now relax and stop doing schoolwork. They reason to themselves that they have passed the apex of the mountain or the halfway mark of the school year, so the journey is just about complete. Some students believe that it will be just a matter of sliding downhill to the flatlands on the other side of the mountain. In other words, they figure they don't have to put forth any more effort in their schoolwork.

This could not be further from the truth. A good mountain climber uses specific techniques to safely rappel down to the base camp from the mountain peak, and only then is the journey complete. The same thing is true for the school year. There are still test benchmarks to be met. Targeted teaching and learning must continue to occur after testing, for students to masterfully demonstrate all the concepts they have learned that year.

The general consensus among some students, when the standardized testing is completed, is that the school year is over. These students - luckily, they are in the minority - will test the teacher's patience. They might say, 'Testing is over. Why do we still have to do schoolwork?" or "Why can't we just relax and have some fun?" Their whining and complaining begin to sound like a broken record and can frustrate even the most seasoned veteran teacher. Some students refuse to do homework, do not participate in class discussions, and will not even attempt to complete written assignments for class. How should a teacher address this?

First of all, I gently remind my students that they are currently in school and that the school year runs from September to June. I admit that yes, standardized testing is over, and every day we are moving closer to the end of the year, but the key word here is "school". I remind them that school is not over until June and that there are still other types of assessments to be administered. I break it down in simple terms to them: that although one important formative assessment is over, there are still other benchmarks to be met periodically and that there is a summative assessment coming up at the end of the year. I also remind them that we have several weeks to go before that occurs. In the meantime, I conclude in my appeal to them that as we continue to teach and learn, I can and will tailor the instruction to include more hands-on activities.

This usually satisfies the majority of the students. However, be aware that there are always some who will try to challenge your authority during the last few months of school. Do not despair, however, because there are a wide variety of student-centered strategies for presenting the curriculum that are guaranteed to capture the imagination of even the most jaded student. **(See Appendix 5 - Appendix 7.)**

One of the ways I appease my students is to remind them of the fact that field trips will be coming up soon. Most students enjoy going on trips, and parents are generally supportive, especially when they do not have to pay. In areas commonly referred to as the "inner city", many companies sponsor field trips for students who are deemed to be underprivileged. Trips to museums, botanical gardens, aquariums, and zoos are typical for most school districts and are avenues for great learning experiences. Teachers can be sure that their students will be booked to attend field trips to at least one of these popular destinations, and the skillful teacher will incorporate group projects into these activities. In this way, students will experience interactive learning without the constraints of being in the classroom all day.

A particular field trip that stands out in my memory was to Washington, DC. I was assigned to spearhead a trip during which I would chaperone students to the Supreme Court and other places of national interest, located in the nation's capital. As I prepared them for the trip, we spent many hours learning the history of the US Supreme Court and the biography of the current Justices. Our group was scheduled to meet with Justice Elena Kagan, the fourth female Supreme Court Justice since its inception in 1789, and so we focused on her life story.

Unfortunately, Justice Kagan had an emergency that caused her to cancel our meeting. However, she sent a representative, and we were able to sit in the Supreme Court and see the seat where the current President, Barack Obama, sat whenever he visited the US Supreme Court. What a fun day that was! Having a class trip to a courthouse and visiting a courtroom, whether on the municipal, county, or state level, children get firsthand experience and knowledge of our justice system and learn how it works. Our trip also included visiting the new Martin Luther King Jr. monument.

During the actual trip, students were guided to take note of specific information and places and to ask well-thought-out questions of the various tour guides. After returning to school, students worked together in small groups to create a visual interpretation of their visit to Washington D.C. This project was counted as a major Social Studies and English Language Arts grade for the marking period. However, the experience of traveling to the nation's capital on a school trip was an invaluable life experience that they will not easily forget. Every new teacher will not be assigned to such an elaborate trip, but teachers can arrange memorable field trips for their students.

Another way a teacher can diversify his/her instruction is by having class instruction outdoors. One of my most cherished childhood memories of school days - from elementary to secondary - is when we had lessons outdoors. It did not happen every day, but it was magical when it did. The mere prospect of it happening from time to time filled me with joyful anticipation. If going outside is not an option in your situation, maybe you could plan an afternoon of learning in the library or the auditorium. Changing the location of the instruction can help capture and hold your students' attention. Whatever you decide to do to diversify learning, it is important for students to understand that school is still in session and learning must continue.

At this time of year, I also get my students involved in a unit of planning performing arts-type projects, which they will perform toward the end of the school year. It is important for them to play a major role in planning this type of project, so that they will buy into the eventual successful performance as a reward for their hard work. It is important for students to participate in kinesthetic learning. This unit/project can be done in such a clever way that the students do not realize that they are working hard and meeting the required core curriculum state standards. A project can be incorporated into any subject area. This is a great avenue for showcasing your students' learning, and quantify their growth from the beginning of the school year.

One example of incorporating project-based learning or PBL is to use the ELA material studied in a particular unit and incorporate it into a play. One year, my seventh-grade class worked on a Language Arts/Social Studies unit titled, *Stolen Childhoods*. We read about school-age children in various parts of the world who do not go to school because they are the victims of forced child labor. We read about some of the children who were mere infants - not yet potty trained - when they started working in forced child labor. Some children were chained so that they would stay in one place as they worked for up to 16 hours a day working as migrant laborers in the fields, making soccer balls, weaving rugs, and working in diamond mines.

I designed a unit in which the students read and analyzed the text, then they researched child labor in the United States and compared the information from the ELA text with present-day situations in the United States. Taking it a step further, they demonstrated comprehension and mastery by writing plays/vignettes to illustrate various scenarios of child labor, both overseas and in the USA. The students had so much vested interest in the project that they were willing to stay before and after regular school hours to practice and perfect their scenes. The project culminated in an assembly program that showcased their work, to which parents, school district personnel, and community members were invited.

That was a win-win-win situation. Students had the opportunity to demonstrate their knowledge and skills, parents were able to see first-hand what their children had learned at school, while the principal and the school district superintendent glowed with pride. Everyone does not like to be in the spotlight on stage, so we found roles for every student, and each child contributed to the production. Some students were stage managers and others assistant directors; some students were in charge of costumes, curtains, lighting, and sound. They became a well-oiled machine that worked together for the good of the class, and the assembly was a resounding success. In this way, we were able to celebrate every child in the class by tapping into their strengths.

Testing Is Over: Now What?

This is just one example of a resultant project from a unit of study in English Language Arts (ELA). Math projects can include demonstrations of students' mental math agility such as Math Jeopardy, Math Riddles, or Math Architect, designing a fun structure using Math information. For '

Social Studies and Science, students can choose a unit of study and, in small groups, prepare information to present to the class. This can also be portrayed during an assembly. The ideas are unlimited for class projects. Students will have fun as they spend valuable time researching information to incorporate into their projects while meeting the core curriculum state standards.

Another activity that will be sure to pique the interest of students is to be the associate teacher for the day. The student will have the opportunity to prepare and actually teach a lesson. They will have a *bona fide* experience of what it is like to be the teacher, and will be able to empathize with the teacher afterward. During the lesson, the other students are required to address that student-teacher as if they were the actual teacher, and he/she will have autonomy to the extent of questioning the classroom teacher to check for comprehension while the associate teacher is teaching the lesson. This invaluable first-hand experience is guaranteed to have a major impact on students. It is something that a student-teacher will cherish for many years to come.

There are countless ELA project-based activities, one of which is for students to create a new game and write the rules of the game. This project could incorporate Math, Social Studies, and Science as well, depending on the game. It could be an individual assignment, or the teacher might assign the students to work in pairs or small groups. Imagine the hours of research, reporting, trial and error, and triumphs this would entail. Imagine the students' pride and joy as they showcase their project at a special school fair! Teachers and students are only limited by their imagination as they engage in project-based learning in the latter part of the school year. It will take more time and effort to plan and implement project-based learning units, but it will be beneficial for student learning and experience, and it will be well worth the effort.

Chapter 10

Celebrate the Students in Several Ways

Each child does not progress at the same pace, nor does every child excel in every subject area. Consequently, each child's progress must be recognized and rewarded. It is important for the teacher to make everyone feel important and acknowledged. The teacher must be the biggest cheerleader for the students, especially at the end of the school year. Therefore, it is so important to celebrate students in different ways. As educators, we never know the full potential of the students in our class, but we know that every child is important, so we must treat them as if they will all go on to become super stars in one field or another. Many people who became famous as adults were once overlooked in elementary, middle, or high school, and that is unfortunate. Teachers must take their profession seriously. As educators, we touch the future forever, because teaching is the only profession upon which all other professions depend.

Teachers are not perfect. We do not always get it right. Sometimes we make a mistake, misdiagnose a person's character, and out of frustration and anger, we may sometimes say negative and hurtful things to a student. When that student grows up and becomes a phenomenal success, I would be willing to bet that the teacher who spoke negatively about their student's life is saddened and deeply embarrassed. I can imagine them wringing their hands in regret and shame for the words they spoke about that child many years ago. And then there are caring teachers who go the extra mile or two to ensure the success of their students. You must decide for yourself what kind of teacher you want to be, and work toward that goal. Take, for example:

- Richard Branson, whose headteacher told him that he would most likely end up in prison. He is now a business tycoon and commercial astronaut in England, the owner of The Virgin Group, which controls more than 400 companies today.

- Thomas Edison's teachers told him that he was too stupid to learn anything. He is now regarded as one of the most successful inventors who ever lived, having held more than 1,000 patents. His creations have affected the entire world.

- Albert Einstein did not start speaking until he was four and did not learn to read until he was seven. It was widely thought that he was mentally handicapped. Einstein most likely had caring teachers who took the time to work with him painstakingly until he was able to excel on his own. Today, his name is synonymous with intelligence. A good, caring teacher encourages students and facilitates learning.

Teachers stand *in loco parentis* when students are in our care. As such, we try to instill good qualities in our students, and hope they remember to persevere when the hard times come. When, like Oprah Winfrey, they are told at a young age that they are not fit to be on TV because they present the wrong image, they are able to dig into their stockpile of determination and pride that has been accumulating throughout their years of schooling, and forge forward to international success. They may even face adversity like Sidney Poitier, who grew up in poverty, and was told at his first film audition to "stop wasting everyone's time and get a job as a dishwasher or something." Because of the grit and determination that had been sown into him by his parents and teachers, he went on to win an Academy Award, and was awarded the Presidential Medal of Freedom. Sidney Poitier is regarded as one of the best male actors of all time.

Not all children will not grow up to be a celebrity, but every child can excel in their own way, and at their own pace. And that is where a good teacher comes in. A teacher is required to find creative ways to celebrate her/his students for their efforts throughout the year. Something as simple as a call home to inform the a student's parent that they did well at school that day can be a powerful dose of encouragement for that child, and will help curry favor with the parents. My philosophy is that we (teachers) call home from time to time to alert parents to their children's inappropriate behavior at school. Our communication with parents should not end there. We should make doubly sure to report on the good things that students are doing. Let parents share in the joys and triumphs of their children. After all, they are partners in education with teachers, so involving them and keeping them informed of their children's progress is an excellent idea. Communication is a great way to bond with your parents.

There is a lot to be said about verbally praising a student for a job well done. Flattery is never recommended, Nothing worthwhile will be accomplished that way. The truth is that the children can see you right through you when you are insincere. However, children thrive on verbal encouragement from their teacher. There are times when the teacher's words are more important to a child than the word of their parents. I have proved this to be true over the years, hence the importance of being sincere and intentional in interactions with our students. Sometimes a teacher might have to look a little harder to find something to compliment a child on, but it could mean the world to that child to get a kind word of encouragement from their teacher. A teacher must find a way to create and maintain an inclusive environment in the classroom, and that means reaching out with positivity to every child, because they all need to feel a sense of self-worth and of belonging.

Just as with the verbal compliment to the child and parents, a teacher can celebrate her/his students by sending a note home to parents or via email. Once again, this keeps the channel of communication open. It keeps parents in the loop of what is happening in the classroom, and tells how their child is making strides educationally. When parents know that you are sincere, they will do anything to cooperate with you. When a child sees the parent and teacher working together, he/she is encouraged to cooperate in class and might achieve even higher grades. This is a win-win-win situation, in which everyone is happy - child, teacher, and parent.

Another great way to celebrate your students is to have a class-wide celebration. This could take many formats, but most importantly, the principal and your direct supervisor must be aware of and approve your plans. Once you have passed that hurdle, the next step is to get the students involved. You could include parents, depending on the time of day and the type of celebration you are planning. It might be something as simple as extra recess time because the class has met a particular goal, or it could be as elaborate as going to see the Rockettes performance of the Nutcracker at Radio City Music Hall in New York City, to celebrate meeting a major challenge.

A school-based celebration could be a pizza party in the class during the last period of the day. It could also be a movie afternoon in which the time block after lunch to the end of the day is devoted to watching a celebratory movie. Whether it is a simple or elaborate affair depends on the teacher and the reason for the reward. Whatever the class-wide celebration entails, children must be involved in the planning and execution, to create a meaningful and cherished memory.

Throughout the school year, students' work can be celebrated through displays in the classroom and hallway. Whenever parents see their children's, work prominently displayed, it elicits a sense of pride and appreciation. Every child's work will not receive an A grade, but when a child applies himself and does their best, the teacher deserves to recognize their efforts. When you acknowledge a child's hard work, he/she will be encouraged to continue to work hard, with the aim of achieving an even better grade in the next cycle. The teacher must be the most vociferous and enthusiastic cheerleader for the students. As the child progresses, it is important that the teacher creates various ways to celebrate the successes.

Certificates continue to be a great way to celebrate progress. They do not have to be elaborate but must be authentic. Do not give a child a certificate if it is not earned. That would be perpetrating a fraud, and would do more harm than good to the student. You can create your own generic certificates for whatever unit you are studying, or you can buy store-bought ones that are more general.

In either case, certificates can be used throughout the year to reward students. You may decide to award certificates monthly, or once per marking period. The choice is yours. However, be intentional about the frequency when you start, because if you decide to do them too often, it can become an overwhelming chore for you after a while. Additionally, certificates might not mean as much to students if they are awarded too frequently. Some teachers present a certificate to the Student of the Week. I highly recommend Student-of-the-Month certificates.

The awards assemblies each marking period are school-wide celebrations of students' efforts. The highest-achieving students are generally rewarded in the categories of Principal's List, Super Honor Roll, Honor Roll, and Honorable Mention. There are very strict grading rules that allow students to receive awards in each of these categories. High achievers have worked hard and deserve to be rewarded, and the teacher is very proud of them. But what about the others? This is when the teacher can become creative in celebrating other hard-working students for their efforts.

At the risk of sounding repetitive, every student will not be an A student, but if a child tries his/her best, there must be a way to celebrate him/her during the grade-level Awards Assembly. I was raised to believe that as long as you are doing your best, no one can do better than that. Once you recognize a child's best efforts, it is time to stand up for him/her and present that child with a reward for the marking period. It could be a Certificate of Completion, Most Improved Student, Certificate of Recognition, or Good Citizen Certificate. These certificates show recognition of their great efforts, although they may not be the best academically performing students. The number and types of awards will be determined by the teacher, but it is important for children to be rewarded for their efforts in more categories than those stipulated for receiving the highest academic honors.

Imagine the pride that a child feels when called up on stage to receive an award! That could possibly be the encouragement that he/she needs to go to a higher academic level. And if we can provide students with the incentive to perform better during the next marking period and beyond, why not? What would be the harm in encouraging a child to challenge himself/herself? Many of our students go through difficult issues at home, some of which we, as adults, have never experienced. If being appreciated at school can help shine a glimmer of light in their dark world, then by all means we should leap at the opportunity to do so. I am not in any way, shape, or form, advocating for hollow or sham rewards. That would be completely pointless, inappropriate, and even cruel. I am simply appealing to educators to give our students hope, which is sadly lacking in many of their lives.

To sum it all up, teachers are called to be and do many things for their students throughout the school year. We are required to deliver the curriculum every day, and to ensure that learning is taking place in our classrooms. However, as a novice teacher, one of the most important things you can do for your students is to celebrate them periodically and in various ways. As mentioned at the beginning of this book, every student is an individual with their own distinct personality, so there must be different ways to celebrate them.

As your year progresses, you will determine which celebrations are best for your group of students. You might decide to try one or more of the suggested activities discussed in this book, or devise one of your own. There is no hard and fast rule about celebrating your class; however, you must get the approval of your supervisor in advance. Once that person is on board, there is nothing stopping you from creating meaningful and memorable celebrations that your students will carry with them for the rest of their lives.

Chapter 11

Everybody Wins - In the Home Stretch

As the days go by, it becomes more and more difficult for students to sit still in the classroom and focus on teacher-centered lessons. Teachers can continue to create innovative ways to engage students, especially as they approach the end of the year. These lessons can be even more concrete and meaningful than the strategies discussed in Chapter 9. At this point, it is about a month before the end of the school year. Teachers can continue to help students feel excited about coming to school by involving them in hands-on, whole-class activities. In this way, everybody wins.

An example of this would be for the class to create a book together. In these days of digital technology, that would not be a difficult task. It is a tangible way for students to see their collaborative achievements, and provide them with another memory to cherish, and eventually share with their children and grandchildren. Every child is not a great reader or writer, but every child knows how they feel at any given time. As such, each student can write a poem. It may be short and does not have to rhyme, but a poem can record the poet's feelings, either in a few or many words. If a poem is all the children can contribute to the class book project, then that is sufficient. The poem does not have to be about feelings. It could be about weather, about a school event, about their family members, or about someone/something in their community. Again, the topics can be wide-ranging and are limited only by the writer's imagination.

I have completed the whole-class book writing project, and it is richly rewarding for both the teacher and students. The creation of the book is a cathartic experience for some students, and it provides closure for others. The actual writing sessions are filled with collaboration from some of the least likely students as they team up unofficially and help edit each other's work. I have seen new friendships formed and alliances made at this time. When the writing and editing are completed, and the book is finally printed and bound, the look of joy and pride on their faces is indescribable. It is well worth the time and effort required to facilitate this project.

When the book is published, another idea for celebrating your whole class is to have your students share excerpts of their literary skills as documented in the printed book. For this occasion, you will work with your class to decorate and transform the classroom into an inviting space. You will formally invite parents in for a Literary/Poetry Café, or a Poetry Slam on a specific date and time. I guarantee this will be an unforgettable experience for both the students and their parents.

Another great ELA end-of-year project is the culmination of a mock trial event. The New Jersey State Bar Foundation sponsors a yearly mock trial competition for students at various levels of schooling - elementary, middle, and high school categories. Other states probably offer similar projects. At the beginning of the school year, students can brainstorm ideas to create court cases based on events in the news or purely from their imagination. Teachers must officially register their school for the mock trial competition by the registration deadline, a few weeks after the start of the school year.

Once the school is registered in the fall, the class must revisit their court case(s) periodically and complete the writing and submission in order to be considered for the competition. The case entry deadline is at the end of January of the current school year, and the results are published by the end of April. At this point, classes with the winning cases in each grade level should start practicing their cases and prepare to present them in front of the judge and lawyers at the New Jersey State Bar Foundation. Even if a case does not win an award from the Foundation, the teacher can celebrate her students by having them do a school-based performance for their peers. This can be an exciting event, since the audience members will become the jury and decide whether the plaintiff or the defendant made a stronger case.

The mock trial has been a mainstay in my ELA classes for years. It is a means of building up students' self-confidence and broadening their horizons by exposing them to like-minded students from other school districts throughout the state. Over the years, I have seen firm friendships formed from students interacting with others whom they have met in this forum. I am gratified to be able to orchestrate these experiences for my students who would otherwise only communicate with fellow students from their own school and district in the inner city.

As the year draws closer to end, a skilled teacher will capitalize on the strengths of his/her students through debates. This practice should be started at the beginning of the school year and engaged in periodically throughout the year. Whether it is simply done in the classroom centered around the current unit of study or by participating in a debate league, debating creates an outlet for students to express themselves and let their voices be heard.

The core curriculum standards for ELA are met and solidified through debate. As a teacher of ELA and a debate coach for many years, I can attest to the myriad benefits of this activity. In addition to honing their research skills, building self-confidence, and allowing students to grow academically and socially, debate teaches metacognition. Students become aware of their own thought processes as they engage in a round of debate. They are constantly thinking about the strength of their arguments and how they can be effectively presented.

An important aspect of debate is that it opens the door to higher education. When an elementary and middle school debater pursues debating in high school, they are given the opportunity to travel throughout the country debating in various venues, usually prestigious universities, and meeting other debaters to whom they would not otherwise be exposed. It allows them to broaden their circle of friends as they interact with other students nationally and builds their self-confidence as they become experienced debaters and travelers.

Students are currently offered debate scholarships to Rutgers University, one of the most highly respected universities in the country. I have had debate students who were awarded full debate scholarships. This shows how important it can be to incorporate debate into your classroom. There is a popular saying, "A journey of a thousand miles begins with the first step." Engaging in debate may be the first step in a lifelong journey for some students, but it is a worthwhile step. As educators, we are called to expose our students to as many positive activities as possible.

Each student will not opt to pursue debate in a league, but some will, and they will reap the benefits. Anecdotal research suggests that debating helps students improve their overall academic grades. I have had several shy students who became confident public speakers because of their participation in debate. As students become more adept at researching and presenting their case, they become better listeners. This is a necessary debate skill in preparation for the rebuttal of their opponents' arguments. Active listening is a lifelong skill that is essential for success in whatever field the student decides to pursue after completing his/her schooling. One never knows what doors may be opened for students in the future if they are introduced to the challenges and joys of debate today, so I encourage you to make debating a part of your classroom projects.

There are other activities to consider incorporating into your planning as the end of the school year approaches. One such assignment is a scavenger hunt based on a particular unit of study. This way, your lesson plans meet the required state curriculum standards, and your students are fully engaged. For the scavenger hunt, students read and follow clues to find hidden objects related to the unit. This may sound simple and mundane, but success depends on reading and understanding the directions as a group and collaborating before proceeding with the hunt. This idea is not limited to ELA. A scavenger hunt can be tailored to any subject area and will require students to strategize and work collaboratively in groups or pairs to achieve success.

Another great idea combines ELA with science and possibly mathematics. After working on a specific unit, or after reviewing all units covered so far for the year, students work in groups to "invent" a new product that will benefit humanity. They will be required to give a detailed explanation of the purpose of their invention and how it works. To incorporate technology, students are required to create an online/TV advertisement demonstrating the benefits of their invention. The students have autonomy over the format of their advertisement, but the teacher must approve the premise of it in advance, and must preview the video before presenting it to an audience.

A great social studies unit that can be combined with ELA is for students to learn the history of their school, town, county, or state and create a brochure to promote it. A creative teacher can find a way to incorporate all of this. The class could be assigned four different areas of pursuit with respect to the brochure, and depending on the size of the class, there may be more than one group working on each topic. Imagine the excitement of your students as they delve into the history of their assigned subject and engage in discussions to categorize the importance of information gleaned from their research! Students will have to utilize all their group work strategies as they proceed with the planning and execution of their video advertisement. Once again, they will be fully engaged while meeting the state curriculum standards.

As we enter the home stretch of the school year, it is imperative that teachers become more creative in planning and executing lessons that will capture and hold the attention of their students. This does not mean that the students must sit and be stationary for the entire time. In 1983, Harvard developmental psychologist, Howard Gardner, espoused the theory of various types of learning. His theory of multiple intelligences suggests that human intelligence can be categorized as the following: visual-spatial, verbal-linguistic, musical-rhythmic, logical-mathematical, interpersonal, intrapersonal, naturalistic, and bodily-kinesthetic. In other words, we all learn differently.

That is why it is important for students to be exposed to more than one form of learning. Clearly, everyone is an individual with their own learning style. Varying the way lessons are presented optimizes learning, and becomes a win-win situation in the classroom: the students are more fully engaged in the lesson at hand, and the teacher has less disciplinary issues and becomes more of a facilitator than a lecturer. If a child is fully engaged, he/she has no time to be disruptive, so I encourage you to vary your teaching strategies for the benefit of everyone involved.

Bridget Samuel Charles

Chapter 12

It's So Hard To Say Goodbye

Saying goodbye to classmates can be difficult for many students, so it is important for the teacher to create ways to help ease the withdrawal process. Preparing a memory book is a great way to have students memorialize their year together. For one reason or another, some children will never return to that town after the school year is over. While most of the students will remain in the local school district, others will move to another city, state, or country. A memory book with the autographs of classmates is a great keepsake for a child to take with them. The teacher should autograph each child's book and include a few words of wisdom to provide future inspiration for that child.

Some people might think that a memory book would be too juvenile for anyone, except elementary students. However, that is not true. Everyone likes to be remembered and to be reminded of their friends. That is why there are graduation year books at the end of 12th grade. A memory book is a tailored version of the yearbook. There may or may not be pictures, but it is a means of preserving the people and events from a particular year. The memory book helps the student keep the friendships and accomplishments from that specific year fresh in mind. Whenever they review the memory book, most people smile as they reminisce about what used to be.

Creating a memory book is also a reflection of the teacher. Students remember teachers who take the time to create an instrument that enables them to preserve their class memories. It is not difficult to do this, especially these days with the advanced technology that is so rampant. The teacher can have the class brainstorm some of the fun, exciting events that occurred during the year and then vote on the ones they would like included in the book. Of course, students should have the opportunity to record their own personal favorite event in their individual memory book, as well as an event they recall that involved the person whose book they are signing. Every memory book should have ample space for autographs. I usually allot at least two pages (front and back of each), for autographs. Students want to collect as many autographs as possible to remember their classmates and cool personnel at the school.

The cover of the Memory Book should have space for the student to attach their picture. They should also fill out important information on the cover page such as the student's name and grade, the name and address of the school, and the current school year. Information inside the Memory Book should include:
- A Day in the Life of...
- School Favorites...
- Books Read...
- Subjects and Special Areas...
- Field Trips...
- A Special Event That Occurred This Year...
- About My Teacher...

A Memory Book is one of the best gifts a teacher can give to her students at the end of the year.

Another great way to remember your year is to create a digital success video on-screen that highlights important events from the school year. This video will be a compilation of special moments throughout the school year and will include snippets inclusive of everyone. All students might not be prominently featured in the video, but everyone should see him-/herself at some point on the screen doing something positive. This project will require some foresight and careful planning, but the extra time and effort are worth it. Students will be beaming ecstatically as they recognize themselves in various scenarios that would possibly have been forgotten if not for the video.

This project can be collaborative in that the teacher assigns a video/picture taking committee that will operate on special occasions, and not during the core curriculum subjects. Students can capture videos during trips, rallies, and special competitions as the year progresses. As they watch the culmination of their efforts at the end of the year, it will elicit strong emotion, and help children remember their caring teacher and the special way she/he made them feel that year.

Children can use the time at the end of the year to write letters to students who will be in their homeroom next year. Their letters will follow the guidelines provided by the teacher, but they will have some latitude to give advice to their younger counterparts. This will be your current students' opportunity to be most sagacious in guiding the younger students, since they have already "been there and done that". Writing this letter enables the teacher to appreciate the students' growth in writing, as they use the literary skills and techniques practiced since September. It also allows the student to become an expert writer and giver of advice.

Over the years, my students have enjoyed this activity. They take the time to think carefully before writing this letter, and they give sound advice. The letters usually remind new students to follow the class rules or face the consequences of the teacher who "does not play" when it comes to respect. Current students also remind future students to always do their homework and classwork on time. They usually stress the fun they had that year, and that made me realize that despite the fact that I had to be a strict disciplinarian, the students appreciated my efforts to help mold their character. I believe that you will have similar experiences with your students.

As mentioned above, teaching a lesson held outside the building can be rewarding. Students appreciate learning in a different environment from time to time. An activity that can be carried out in the open air is the art of oral storytelling. Students of West African descent will appreciate learning that many stories in the black culture have been passed down by word of mouth from generation to generation. Students from other cultures will also find after research that most cultures include some form of storytelling, either within the family or as a community. Story telling is as old as time.

The teacher can plan a unit in which students research their culture online and interview their parents and grandparents. Then they would choose a story from their cultural tradition to present to the class. Stories can be told in small group settings, with the listeners in each case grading the story on a rubric. The student in each group that receives the highest grade has the opportunity to perform in a special forum outside in the fresh air. As he/she performs for the entire class, the child is graded on a rubric. When the winner from each group has relayed his/her story and the scores are tallied, the child with the highest scores overall is deemed the Official Storyteller of the Class. This would be a noteworthy event to record in the memory book, and the video squad would take pictures and/or videos for inclusion in the success video.

Letters are a great way to let others know how you feel about them. Another worthwhile letter-writing activity involves writing a thank you to various members of staff. Students interact with many staff members in addition to the teacher. The African saying "It takes a village to raise a child" is apropos in this situation. Many members of staff have invested in the success of your students, and it would behoove you to encourage the students to show their gratitude. Students could possibly write thank-you letters to the following school workers:

- Custodian
- Librarian
- School Nurse
- Cafeteria worker
- Security Guard
- Social Worker
- Vice Principal
- Principal
- Activity teachers

These end-of-year activities are beneficial to the students in several ways. They allow students to work in a variety of forums and to showcase their work. They provide closure to the work that has been done all year. They allow students and teachers to continue to meet the core curriculum content standards as they explore multiple intelligences and engage in a more kinesthetic style of learning. Above all else, these varied activities allow students to demonstrate how much they have learned since the beginning of the school year.

It is hard to say goodbye on the last day of school, but it must be done. Will you become emotional? Of course, you will, and that's fine. However, you must try your best to stay strong for the sake of the children. They will need you to be the tower of strength that they have come to depend on over the course of the school year. If a tear slips out, wipe it quickly. and keep your demeanor as cool as possible. If a child sees you wiping your eyes, that is fine. We are all human. Please don't break down completely with loud uncontrollable sobs and rivers of tears.

The school year is over, and you will miss your students, but there will be a fresh batch of students to teach and learn from next year. You will love them just as much or even more than you loved this year's group. Yes, your current students will hold a special place in your heart because they were your first homeroom class, but you will survive the separation and so will they. Comfort yourself with this thought.

Children take their cues from adults, so on this last day with your students, set a good example for them and try not to break down. Think about the good times you had together during the past year. Remember the laughter and joy that you shared as a group. These positive memories will help you through the emotions you will experience that day. Before you know it, the last day will be over. You will have said your goodbyes, and will go home feeling sad, but relieved. You survived! You will come to the full realization that you made it through your first year of teaching, and your joy will be rekindled. Congratulations!

Chapter 13

You Did It! It's Time to Celebrate You

As you reflect on the recently completed school year, give yourself some grace. You had some challenges and made some mistakes, but you have also discovered some awesome areas of strength within yourself that you must now take time out to celebrate. Take the time to acknowledge your areas of challenge, and to celebrate your achievements. But before you do that, take some time to rest. Luxuriate in the fact that you do not have to wake up at the crack of dawn, as the alarm clock shrieks its shrill command to wake up and start your day. You can sleep for as long as you wish every day, for the next two months or so. Let that thought sink into your consciousness, and when you have rested a little while, come back to the topic of your school year and analyze it.

You will reminisce about the entire school year, starting with your first day in September, and proceeding to the recently concluded last day of school in June. As you think about September, you will most likely realize that all the pedagogy you learned in the university in preparation for teaching, could not fully prepare you for the on-the-job training you received from working directly with the students.

Thinking back to the first day, you might revisit your trepidation as you waited for the students to line up at their designated area, and then you will smile as you realize you had no need to worry. You will acknowledge that as long as you did your introductions and created the class rules on the first day, you were well on your way to taking control of your class. You will also revisit the early days when you established your rituals and routines. It took some practice, and a couple of reset days when you had to revisit the rules and regulations, but the students finally caught on. Some even became unofficial teacher's helpers in that they reminded their classmates about what to do when they lagged in complying with the current command of "STAR!" or "HALL!". You will acknowledge how invaluable those strategies were in establishing discipline and redirecting the students' attention.

Thinking about your year as a classroom teacher, you will most likely smile as you recount the realization that every child has a voice that must be heard, whether in writing, or in discussions. You will marvel at all you learned about your students individually and as a group. You learned quickly which students were bossy, and which were reticent. You might even reminisce about the strategies that you used to hear everyone's point of view: strategies like periodic debate sessions, the use of Reading Circles, or by engaging in Think-Pair-Share and Idea Wave during small group or whole group instruction.

Continuing to stroll down Memory Lane, you will be grateful for having learned that familiarity breeds contempt, and that is why students should be made to observe boundaries regarding physical interactions with the teacher. Realizing that even the hint of inappropriate behavior toward your students could result in allegations and cause you to lose your job, you are grateful for the Safe Sanctuaries training you received. This training helped you to avoid accusations of physical or sexual impropriety. Being a caring teacher, you resolve that during the next year of teaching, you will acknowledge your love for your students, and your willingness to help them be successful. However, you will make the decision to always obey the guidelines provided, regarding physical interactions between teachers and students. In other words, you will love them from an appropriate distance.

One of the greatest lessons you will have learned over the past year was the importance of parents. You studied the topic of parent-teacher relationships during teacher-training classes, but as it became a reality, you realized how crucial it was to have good relationships with the parents of your students. This year, you learned first-hand how your parent allies can help smooth your way throughout the school year, or not. Their cooperation with you was dependent on the relationship you formed with them, based on mutual respect and trust. You discovered first-hand that parents are true partners with you in the education of our students. In short, you understood clearly the value of parents in the education system, and you count your blessings for the cooperative ones you had.

As you continue to ruminate on your first year, you will be thankful for the relationships that developed between you and your colleagues, especially the relationship with your mentor. You appreciate every nugget of wisdom shared by that person to aid you in your professional growth. You make a mental note to write a thank-you letter to your mentor to show your appreciation. You consider all the other teachers and staff who poured advice and positive energy into you this past year, and you say an internal thank you, realizing how much more difficult your life would have been without their advice and support. From the custodian to the security guard, from the librarian, to the vice principal and the social worker, you relive some of the incidents that occurred this year, and you smile in silent acknowledgement of their encouraging words and actions throughout the year.

You review the wisdom you have gleaned from your principal. Whether through one-on-one conversations in the office, or from notes taken during speeches at staff development sessions, you are thankful for it all. You realize you have made some mistakes along the way, by not using the correct protocol at specific times, whether by word or deed, but that is now water under the bridge. You were able to learn from your mistakes, and the principal did not use your inexperience against you.

Because you are coachable, you were able to shift your mindset and accommodate whatever necessary changes were required to ensure your students' success. You kept your actions student-centered. Your principal and/or vice principal were able to note your professional growth from one observation, formal or informal, to another. As you continuously implemented suggested changes, your supervisors reported that they were satisfied with your performance.

In reviewing the week of testing, you understand even more fully the importance of being proactive in your self-care. You realize the challenges that assessments present, and now you feel ready to face them during the next year. You mouth a silent thank you for being able to survive that trying week. You are also filled with gratitude for how well your students cooperated in obeying the testing rules and regulations.

As you continue your journey down Memory Lane, you relive the period after testing, when students became restless and challenging. You were grateful for suggestions on how to engage your students, from more experienced teachers. Of all the ideas you received, you chose the ones you felt would work best with your students, and they did. You smile and reach around to give yourself a pat on the back for making the right choices. You were able to not only survive that period, but to relax and have fun with your students while doing it.

They enjoyed engaging in project-based learning (PBL), and they felt empowered as stakeholders in their own education when they used rubrics to assess their classmates. Your students wrote about many of those positive experiences in their Memory Books, so you are assured that you have touched the future through the efficacious engagement of your skills and techniques with your students during your first year of teaching.

As you come to the end of your rumination on your teaching experience, you reflect on the last day of school and how emotionally charged it was. You recall the hugs and tears of the students. And how they promised to stay in touch with you next year. They lingered so long, it was as if they did not want the day to end; did not want to go home. You smile as you revisit the touching moment when you waved goodbye to the very last student. Knowing that you would not have to obey the command of the alarm clock the next morning or for many mornings to come was powerfully empowering and liberating. You chuckle as you contemplate being able to sleep late the next day.

As you sit quietly and summarize your first year as a classroom teacher, you realize it was worth it. You had many sleepless nights of grading papers and worrying about formal observations the next day, but everything worked out well in the end, and you are looking forward to returning to the classroom next year. You smile as you realize the veracity of the saying, "Today is the tomorrow you worried about yesterday, and all is well." Yes, you tell yourself. All is well indeed. Overall, my first year of teaching and learning turned out fine. I survived. There was no need to worry.

Afterword

Teachers are vitally important in the lives of their students, and rightly so, since they help shape their students' character. Students should also be important to teachers, and thankfully, this is true for the most part. Unfortunately, some teachers do not provide a nurturing environment in their classroom. They do not seem to realize that one day the small children sitting in front of them will grow up to become adults, and will remember how their teachers treated them, and how they made them feel. Maya Angelou said it best when she said, "People will forget what you said, people will forget what you did, but people will never forget how you made them feel."

Teachers will not become rich from their salary. At times, their efforts to educate the youth might seem to go unnoticed and unappreciated by those in authority, but they should never lose heart. Their rewards will come in the academic achievements of their students, and the life lessons they are able to help instill in them. Teachers have a great responsibility. Touching the future every day, they reflect the human side of education. That is why it is so important to create a nurturing and safe environment in classrooms, and to care about every single child they service.

I can only speak for myself, but I want my students to have fond memories of me. I want them to remember me as the kind of teacher who went the extra mile to educate them. I want them to think of me and remember that I was firm, but in a loving and caring way. I want them to remember me as the kind of teacher who laid down the law, but was patient and kind. The teacher who gave her all to her students on many levels, regardless of their status in society, and who did her best to help them learn, not just academic subjects, but the important things in life, like treating others the way you want them to treat you. Like going out of your way to be kind to others even when they might not be able to repay you, and like welcoming and affirming others who are different in one way or another. I want my students to remember that I encouraged them with my words, and that sometimes even if it was with just a smile or a nod, I was there to inspire them. Above all else, I want my students to know that I did my best, and I hope my best was good enough.

Appendix 1

Ice-Breaker – First Day of School

Introducing: _____

Presented by: _____

Best Friend(s): _____

Favorite Subjects: _____

Favorite Sport(s): _____

Favorite Author: _____

Favorite Movie: _____

She/He wants to be a (n) _____ when she/he grows up, because_____.

Goals for this year: 1) _____
                                 2) _____

She/He is going to have a good year in the ___ grade, because she/he plans to:

_____

_____

If she/he could do one thing to make this world a better place, she/he would:

_____

_____

Appendix 2

Example of Class Rules

1. Be kind and respectful to everyone.
2. Listen carefully and follow directions.
3. Raise your hand and wait to be acknowledged before answering a question.
4. Always walk when moving in the halls.
5. Obey the teacher at all times.

Appendix 3

STAR!

S   **Sit up Straight**

T   **Track the Speaker**

A   **Always be on Task**

R   **Respect the Rules**

Appendix 4

HALL!

H	**Hands at Your Side**
A	**All Eyes Forward**
L	**Lips Zipped**
L	**Legs Walking Safely**

Appendix 5

Think-Pair-Share

Think-Pair-Share (TPS) is a cooperative discussion strategy developed in 1981 by Professor Frank Lyman and his colleagues at the University of Maryland. The three stages of this strategy explains what the students are doing at each stage. TPS is an active learning technique in which students are motivated to participate even if they have little intrinsic interest in the topic. (Lyman, 1982; Marzano & Pickering, 2005)

Think-Pair-Share is a collaborative reading strategy that promotes higher order thinking. Think-Pair-Share differentiates instruction, and gives students the opportunity to discuss ideas without feeling stressed or burdened to justify their thinking. They simply think about the answer and then share and discuss their view along with other group members' ideas in the small group setting.

Instead of working in the class as one whole group, students get a chance to think things through on their own, and then share with a partner or partners in a small group. All members of the group cans see each other. After thinking about the question on their own, students present their individual ideas to others in their small group. One person speaks at a time, while the listeners track the speaker. They use active listening to understand what the speaker is saying. If one student is unable to solve the problem, another group member can most likely explain their answer, thus exposing students to other problem-solving methodologies. The important thing is that each group member gets a chance to present their ideas.

When the group has settled on a final answer, their information is shared with the rest of the class. Although a student may not be the group representative to report their official answer, he/she has participated in answering the question posed to the group, and has engaged in critical and creative thinking, listening, and speaking.

Appendix 6

Idea Wave Teaching Strategy

This strategy is used to share various ideas, and to check for understanding. It involves the entire class. The idea wave can be modified by individual teachers to best suit their needs. The wave begins when one student shares his/her idea and passes the wave on to another student. The Idea wave continues with other students, until several ideas have been shared.

The key to success with this strategy is for every student to be an active listener so that ideas are not replicated. Students can agree or disagree with a previous idea, and then present their own. Even if a student agrees with a point just made, they can build on it by first acknowledging that student's idea, and then extending it even further. If they disagree with the previous point, they must be prepared to rebut the argument after stating their disagreement.

An important point to note is that just like the waves in the ocean, this is a fast-moving activity. Students must be prepared to listen carefully and share one idea usually in 10 seconds or less, using a complete sentence. The time allowed can be adjusted by the teacher, but it should not be much longer, in order to keep the momentum of the wave.

One way to modify the Idea Wave is for groups to share out by "catching the wave". The wave can be imaginary, or it can be a small plush toy or other soft object, with no sharp edges. The teacher designates the first group to start sharing, and passes the wave to them. When they have completed sharing their idea, the group gently tosses/throws the "wave" to another group of their choice, to hear their contribution to the discussion. The new group can only begin speaking after they have "caught the wave". The wave action can be continued until the teacher has decided that a sufficient amount of ideas have been shared in the check for understanding.

Appendix 7

Reading Circles

Also known as Literature Circles, Reading Circles are similar to adult book clubs. However, there is much more structure and rigor in the class room Reading Circles. The clear expectations and modeled behavior by the teacher and student volunteers enable group members to discuss books among themselves. Reading Circles enable students to have thoughtful discussions as they build community by exchanging ideas and exploring teamwork. Students learn to think and speak critically as they interact with the text and each other.

Reading Circles help students appreciate the art of discussing books with their peers. They develop the skill of active listening, since this helps them deepen their understanding of books. Students are given an opportunity to analyze texts, and respond to reading not merely by writing an answer to an open-ended question, but by stating their claim on a particular topic, and providing arguments and evidence to support it. In short, Reading Circles help students develop self-confidence, essential comprehension skills through their interactions with each other.

Reading Circles can be used effectively in the classroom when students are given clear directions about what they are required to do. Students must be introduced to the four main jobs of the Reading Circle: **Discussion Director, Literary Luminary, Vocabulary Enricher, and Fact Checker.** When all the roles have been modeled and the students understand the assignment, they participate in discussion with each other, become engaged in reading on a deeper level, and have fun reading.

Appendix 8

PARENT-TEACHER CONFERENCE LOG

Teacher: _____ Grade: _____

School: _____ Room: _____

Student Name: _____

Marking Period: _____

Social: Strengths and Challenges:

Academic: Strengths and Challenges:

Parent Comments:

_____ _____
Parent's Signature   Date

_____ _____
Teacher's Signature   Date

Appendix 9

Debate Practice Form for Multiple Debaters

Date: _____   Judge: _____

1st Affirmative)
(5 pts Maximum each Category)

Evidence   ____
Organization   ____
Cross Examination ____
Delivery   ____
Direct Clash   ____
Total   ____

1st Negative (5
(pts Maximum each Category)

Evidence   ____
Organization   ____
Cross Examination ____
Delivery   ____
Direct Clash   ____
Total   ____

2nd Affirmative
Evidence   ____
Organization   ____
Cross Examination ____
Delivery   ____
Direct Clash   ____
Total   ____

2nd Negative
Evidence   ____
Organization   ____
Cross Examination ____
Delivery   ____
Direct Clash   ____
Total   ____

3rd Affirmative
Evidence   ____
Organization   ____
Cross Examination ____
Delivery   ____
Direct Clash   ____
Total   ____

3rd Negative
Evidence   ____
Organization   ____
Cross Examination ____
Delivery   ____
Direct Clash   ____
Total   ____

4th Affirmative		**4th Negative**	
Evidence	____	Evidence	____
Organization	____	Organization	____
Cross Examination	____	Cross Examination	____
Delivery	____	Delivery	____
Direct Clash	____	Direct Clash	____
Total	____	Total	____
5th Affirmative		**5th Negative**	
Evidence	____	Evidence	____
Organization	____	Organization	____
Cross Examination	____	Cross Examination	____
Delivery	____	Delivery	____
Direct Clash	____	Direct Clash	____
Total	____	Total	____

Affirmative Total Points: ____   **Negative Total Points:** ____

Made in the USA
Middletown, DE
07 March 2024